EARTH CYCLES

ANIMALS

Sally Morgan

W
FRANKLIN WATTS
LONDON•SYDNEY

First published in 2009 by Franklin Watts
Hachette Children's Books
338 Euston Road
London NW1 3BH

Franklin Watts Australia
Level 17/207 Kent Street,
Sydney, NSW 2000

Editor: Jean Coppendale
Design: Paul Manning

Produced for Franklin Watts by
White-Thomson Publishing Ltd

www.wtpub.co.uk
+44 (0) 845 362 8240

A CIP catalogue record for this book is available from the British Library.

ISBN 978 0 7496 8836 3

Dewey classification 590

Picture credits

t = top b = bottom l = left = r = right
1, ECO/Mike Whittle; 3b, 12, Shutterstock/Carrydream; 3r, 9l, Shutterstock/EcoPrint; 4, ECO/Robert Pickett;
5l, Shutterstock/Sergey Kartashov; 5r, Shutterstock/Guentermanaus; 5b, Shutterstock/Christian Musat; 6t, ECO/Reinhard Dirscherl;
6b, 31, Shutterstock/Michelle D. Milliman; 7t, Shutterstock/FloridaStock; 7b, Shutterstock/Eric Gevaert; 7r, ECO/Robert Pickett;
8l, Shutterstock/Peter Betts; 8r, ECO/Fritz Polking; 9b, ECO/Fritz Polking; 9r, ECO/Reinhard Dirscherl; 10t, Shutterstock/Peter
Ingvorsen; 11l, ECO/Robert Pickett; 11r, ECO/Michael Gore; 13t, ECO/John Lewis; 13b, ECO/Neil Miller; 13r, ECO/ Wayne Lawler;
14, ECO/Anthony Cooper; 15l, ECO/Robert Pickett; 15r, Shutterstock/Paul Cowan; 16, ECO/Robert Pickett; 17l, ECO/Robin Redfern;
17r, ECO/John Lewis; 18b, Shutterstock/Angela Hampton; 18t, ECO/Fritz Polking; 19l, Shutterstock/Mark R. Higgins; 19r, ECO/
Frank Blackburn; 20t, ECO/Fritz Polking; 20b, Shutterstock/Cathy Keifer; 21l, ECO/Reinhard Dirscherl; 21r, Shutterstock/Malost;
22l, Shutterstock/SF Photo; 22c, ECO/Robert Pickett; 22r, Shutterstock/Jacob Hamblin; 23l, Shutterstock/Kurt G; 23c,
Shutterstock/Cathy Keifer; 23b, ECO/Robert Pickett; 23r, ECO/Robert Pickett; 24t, ECO/John Liddiard; 24b, Shutterstock/
Anke van Wyk; 25l, ECO/Robert Pickett; 25r, ECO/John Lewis; 26b, Shutterstock/Judex; 27r, Shutterstock/Nick Stubbs;
28l, Shutterstock/Caroline Tolsma; 29l, Shutterstock/Dave Allen Photography; 29r, Shutterstock/Ingvars Birznieks;
29b, Shutterstock/Javarman; 30, Shutterstock/Nagy Melinda. Cover images: ECO/Mike Whittle (main); Shutterstock/
Paul Cowman (egg); ECO/Fritz Polking.

Note to parents and teachers
Every effort has been made by the Publishers to ensure that the websites listed on page 32 are suitable for children, that they are of the highest educational value and that they contain no inappropriate or offensive material. However, because of the nature of the Internet, it is impossible to guarantee that the contents of these sites will not been altered. We strongly advise that Internet access is supervised by a responsible adult.

Printed in China

Franklin Watts is a division of Hachette Children's Books,
an Hachette UK company
www.hachette.co.uk

Contents

Words appearing in **bold** like this can be found in the Glossary on pages 30-31.

What is an animal?

All animals have some **features** in common. For example, they need food to eat so that they can grow, and they can **reproduce**. Unlike plants that make their own food, animals have to find their food in order to survive.

▼ The giant panda is a type of mammal that lives in China. It spends at least 12 hours a day eating bamboo.

Backbones

Animals can be divided into two groups – **vertebrates** and **invertebrates**. Vertebrates are animals with backbones. A backbone is a flexible rod of small bones that runs down the back of animals such as birds, fish and **mammals**. Invertebrates are animals that do not have a backbone. They include insects, **molluscs**, **sea anemones** and worms.

▼ **Reptiles** such as this iguana are vertebrates.

Q Which animal spends its life upside-down?

A The sloth. The sloth is a mammal that lives in the Amazon rainforest in South America. It hangs from branches using its long claws. It eats, sleeps and even gives birth upside-down.

▲ Sloth.

Life cycles

Young animals grow and change into adults. Some changes are gradual, for example a newborn puppy looks like an adult dog, and it gradually gets larger. Other animals go through big changes in appearance. For example, a butterfly **egg** hatches into a **larva**, called a caterpillar. It looks more like a worm than an adult butterfly. The body of the caterpillar has to change to become the adult. This is called **metamorphosis**.

▼ The caterpillar of the swallowtail butterfly.

All types of animals

Animals range in size from tiny animals such as the **amoeba**, which is only a millimetre across, to the blue whale, the world's largest animal, which can grow up to 30 metres long.

▼ Whales are the largest animals. These humpback whales grow to about 15 metres long, and their flippers are one-third of their body length.

Animal species

Scientists have identified about 1.5 million **species** of animals. Each species is unique or different from all other species. But there are many millions of species still waiting to be discovered. These animals live in some of the unexplored habitats of the world, such as remote rainforests and deep oceans.

► This fire-bellied toad is one of 6,400 species of **amphibians**.

Q and A

Animal features

An animal is identified by its features. For example, insects have six legs, while spiders have eight legs. Birds are covered in feathers, and fish are covered in scales. Some animals lay eggs, for example fish and birds, and most mammals give birth to live young.

▲ A bird, such as this bald eagle, is covered with feathers and it has wings instead of arms.

Q What is a fossil?

A A fossil is the preserved remains of an ancient animal or plant. Most fossils, such as the **ammonite** below, are found in rocks and they help scientists to learn about animals that lived millions of years ago, for example the dinosaurs.

▲ Ammonite.

Grouping animals

There are so many animals that scientists put them into groups according to their features. For example, vertebrates are divided into fish, amphibians, reptiles, birds and mammals. Each of these groups is divided into smaller and smaller groups containing fewer species. For example, human beings belong to the **primate** group within mammals. Primates are divided into **lemurs**, monkeys and apes. Humans are a type of ape.

▶ This macaque monkey is a type of primate.

Life of an animal

An animal's life cycle involves birth, growing up, adulthood and death.

Eggs or live young?

Life for all animals begins in an egg. The egg contains the **embryo**, which grows into a young animal. Some female animals lay eggs and these hatch into young, for example insects, fish and birds. Female mammals keep their eggs inside their body. The embryo grows and after a certain period of time, the female gives birth to a baby animal.

Life of mammals

The life cycle of a mammal, such as the lion, starts with the birth of live young. Young mammals rely on their mother for milk. They grow and become adults.

1

▲ A male and female lion come together to mate.

2

▲ A female lion is called a lioness. She gives birth to up to four cubs and feeds the cubs with her milk.

Q and A

Q Which animal can change sex?

A Fish. Many fish found on coral reefs, such as clown fish and wrasses, can change sex. If a large male dies, a female becomes a male to replace him. Scientists are still unsure about how and why this happens. It's one of the mysteries of the reef.

3
▲ The cubs grow quickly. Lions reach adulthood at about 2–3 years of age and are ready to mate.

▲ Clown fish.

Mature mammals

When the adults are mature, they are ready to reproduce and have young of their own. The final stage of the life cycle is the death of the animal. Its body rots and the **nutrients** are usually returned to the ground.

4
▲ Lions in the wild live to about 12 years of age.

Courtship

The first stage in the life cycle of an animal is when the male and female animal pair off. Animals have many ways to attract a mate.

Choosing the best

An animal may choose a mate from their appearance, for example female birds may choose the male with the most colourful feathers. Others pick the male with the best song or the biggest nest. Many male mammals fight other males for females.

▲ Female peacocks choose the males with the longest tail feathers.

▼ These two male wildebeest are fighting over a female. They face each other on their knees and push against each other with their thick horns.

Time of year

Some females can only mate at certain times of year. This may be to ensure that the young are born at a time of year when there is food. Often, the male knows when the time is right by the female's smell or appearance. For example, female butterflies and moths release a smelly substance that the males can detect with their long **antennae**.

Q Which male bird collects gifts to impress a mate?
A The bower bird. The male builds a bower, or nest, to impress the female. It is built from twigs, which the male sticks in the ground. The male bower bird decorates his bower with objects that he finds in the forest and calls to the female to come and look.

female ——

male

▲ Bower birds.

Courting

Some animals carry out a pattern of behaviour called **courtship**, such as a dance or giving gifts. The bird of paradise and the red-crowned crane carry out complex courtship dances. Some male fish also **display** to the female, for example the male stickleback builds a nest and displays in front of it to attract a mate.

◀ Male and female red-crowned cranes pair for life. The pair perform a courtship dance of bows, head-bobbing and leaps.

Reproduction

Reproduction in most animals involves two parents, a male and a female. This is called sexual reproduction.

▼ The male and female butterfly mate. The male butterfly places sperm inside the female to fertilise the eggs.

When animals are ready to reproduce they produce **gametes**. These are special sex cells. The gametes produced by the male are called spermatozoa, or sperm for short. The female produces gametes called eggs. When a male and a female animal mate, the sperm is transferred to the female.

Q and A

Fertilisation

The next stage is **fertilisation**, when a single sperm joins with an egg to produce an embryo. The embryo grows into a new individual. With animals such as fish, fertilisation takes place outside the body of the male and female as the eggs and sperm are released into the water. In animals such as mammals and birds, fertilisation takes place inside the female. Then the female either lays an egg or gives birth to live young.

▼ These angler fish eggs are 4–5 weeks old and have well-developed embryos.

Q Which female eats the male after mating?

A The black widow spider. This spider gets its name because occasionally the female spider eats the male after mating. This happens with other spiders, too, especially the Australian red-back spider. Sometimes the male is eaten because the female mistakes him for **prey**!

▲ Black widow spider.

Asexual reproduction

In a few animals, reproduction occurs without two parents. This is called **asexual reproduction**. All offspring (young) produced asexually are identical to each other and to the parent animal. For example, the amoeba is a tiny **single-celled** animal found in water that reproduces asexually. It simply divides into two and each part grows into a new animal.

buds

▶ The hydra is a small animal that reproduces asexually. This hydra has two buds, which are miniature hydra. They are about to break off.

13

Laying eggs

Most animals lay eggs, except for mammals. A fertilised egg contains an embryo and a store of food, called the yolk. The eggs of fish and amphibians have a protective jelly coat. Reptiles lay eggs with a leathery shell, and birds lay eggs with hard shells. Insects such as butterflies also lay eggs with a shell.

Many or few?

Most fish lay thousands and sometimes millions of eggs. This is because most of the eggs are eaten by other animals. Only a few young fish hatch and grow to adulthood. This means the fish lays many eggs to make sure that some survive. Animals such as birds and reptiles lay fewer, but larger eggs. There is a lot of food in each egg so most of them survive and hatch.

▲ The frog lays its eggs in water. Each egg has a protective jelly coat.

Scattered eggs

Animals that live in water, such as fish, usually scatter their eggs in the water. Some animals bury their eggs in the ground, for example turtles and crocodiles. Most birds lay their eggs in nests where the female bird **incubates** them (keeps them warm) until they are ready to hatch. Butterflies lay their eggs on plants, either singly or in groups.

Q Which bird lays the largest egg?
A The ostrich. The egg of the ostrich weighs about 2 kg and is the equivalent in weight and size to about 24 chicken eggs. An ostrich egg takes an hour to boil!

ostrich egg

chicken egg

▲ The garden snail lays clusters of about 70 to 90 white, round eggs and buries them in the soil.

New life

After a certain length of time, the egg hatches or the female gives birth to her young. The period of time between fertilisation and birth is called the **gestation** period. This can be as short a time as a few weeks in kangaroos, but as long as two years for an elephant.

Hatching

When a chick is ready to hatch, it uses a small tooth on top of its beak to break through the shell and push itself out. It does not need to feed for the first day as it uses up the food stored within its body. Some chicks have fluffy feathers and can run within minutes, but others are born without feathers and are helpless.

▼ This chick has just hatched. It is able to stand up and follow its mother.

Q and A

Giving birth

When the time comes to give birth, female mammals usually move to a safe, sheltered place to have their young. Many give birth at dawn or dusk when there are fewer **predators** around. They may build a nest to keep their young warm.

Q Which male gives birth to young?

A The sea horse. The male and female do a courtship dance, when they wrap their tails around each other. The female lays her eggs in a pouch on the male's **abdomen** where they are fertilised. He keeps the eggs in his pouch for up to four weeks and then the tiny sea horses hatch.

▲ Baby mice are born with no fur, their eyes are closed and they cannot hear. They stay in the nest and feed on their mother's milk.

The eggs are in the male seahorse's pouch.

Litter sizes

Large mammals, such as humans, gorillas and whales, usually give birth to only one baby. Mammals such as cats, dogs and rats give birth to a litter of several babies. Some of the largest litters are born to mice and **opossums**. Tenrecs are small mice-like mammals and they may have as many as 30 babies.

17

Caring for young

Many egg-laying animals simply lay their eggs and leave them, but other animals care for their babies.

Giving milk

All female mammals produce milk to feed their young. Milk is a liquid food that contains all the nutrients needed by the growing mammal. Some new-born mammals feed on milk for just a few days before they start eating solid food. Others feed for much longer. Young elephants, for example, feed on their mother's milk for up to two years.

▲ The grey birds are the chicks of the Emperor Penguin. They have been left together in a **crèche** while their parents hunt for fish.

▼ A newborn lamb stands up within minutes of being born. It is licked dry by its mother and then **suckles** her milk.

Q and A

Feeding young

Growing animals have huge appetites. A blue-tit chick for example, eats 10 caterpillars a day. This means that parent birds spend hours each day finding food for their hungry chicks. Predators such as lionesses and tigers hunt for deer and other herbivores (see page 24) to feed their cubs.

Q Which bird lays its eggs in the nest of other birds?
A The cuckoo. The female cuckoo lays an egg that is similar in colour to the other eggs in the nest. The cuckoo chick hatches first and grows faster and larger than the other chicks. Usually it pushes all the other chicks out of the nest, so it is the only chick and gets all the food.

Guarding babies

Most parents guard their offspring from predators. For example, a herd of musk oxen forms a circle around their calves if wolves come near. Rhinos and elephants attack any animal that threatens their young. Some parent animals will run or fly away, hoping to draw the predator away from where they have left their babies.

cuckoo chick

parent dunnock bird

◀ Kangaroos carry their young, called joeys, around in their pouch where they are protected.

19

Growing up

The next stage in the life of the animal is growing up. Over time, the animal grows larger and becomes an adult animal ready to **breed**.

Learning to hunt

Young predators have to learn how to hunt. If they do not have these skills they will die of hunger. Many mammals, such as cheetahs and lions, learn from their mother. They go with her when she hunts, and when they are large enough they join in.

▲ Play-fighting is very important for young cheetahs. They learn how to fight and hunt without hurting each other.

moulting skin

Getting larger

Reptiles, insects and crabs have a tough **skeleton** around the outside of their body. This causes problems when they grow, because the skeleton does not stretch. This is a bit like wearing clothes that are too small. To grow larger, they must shed their skeleton and grow a new, larger one. This is called **moulting**.

▲ Chameleons have to moult to grow because their scaly skin cannot expand.

Life in the ocean

Many young fish spend the first months of their life as **plankton**, floating in the upper layer of the water. Here they feed and grow. The salmon is unusual because the young salmon hatch in fresh water, but grow to adulthood in salt water and return to fresh water to breed. The turtle lays its eggs in the sand on beaches and a couple of months later the hatchlings emerge. They have to dash to the sea to escape the many birds, crabs and other predators waiting on the beach.

Q Which baby can triple its weight in three weeks?

A An elephant seal pup. The mother's milk is rich in fat so the pup grows quickly for three or four weeks, and a thick layer of **blubber** forms under the skin. When its mother leaves, the young pup has to look after itself. It survives on its blubber while it learns how to catch food.

▲ Elephant seal pup.

▲ Young turtles stay at sea for many years, slowly getting larger. Then they return to the beaches where they were born to breed.

Metamorphosis

Metamorphosis means to change in shape.
This change is an important part of the life cycle
of animals such as amphibians and insects.

The butterfly's life cycle

A butterfly is a type of insect and it has four stages in its life cycle. The adult butterfly lays eggs, which hatch into caterpillars. The caterpillar is the growing stage of the life cycle. Caterpillars feed and grow, and when they reach full size, they moult for the last time and become a **pupa**. Inside the pupa, the body of the caterpillar is rearranged into the body of an adult. When the change is complete, the pupa splits open and a new adult butterfly emerges.

◀ The adult butterfly feeds from flowers and lays its eggs on a leaf.

1

egg

2

caterpillar

Q and A

Q Which tadpole never grows up?

A The axolotl. The axolotl is a type of amphibian. Unlike other amphibians, the tadpole of the axolotl never changes shape when it becomes an adult, but stays as a large tadpole with gills for its entire life. It never undergoes metamorphosis.

3

▼ The case of the pupa splits open and an adult butterfly emerges.

4

pupa

▲ Axolotl.

▼ This tadpole has grown four legs and now its tail will shrink.

Amphibians

Amphibians are animals that live part of their life in water and part on land, for example frogs. The female frog lays her eggs in water where they are fertilised. After a week or so the larvae, called tadpoles, hatch. The tadpoles look a bit like small fish. Over the next couple of months, the tadpoles gradually change in appearance, becoming more like a frog. They grow four legs, their body shape changes and their tail shrinks. Then they are ready to leave the water.

Finding food

Animals cannot make their own food as plants do, so they have to find a ready-made source of food, such as other animals. All the animals and plants living in the same place are **dependent** on each other and they form a **food chain**.

▲ Jellyfish feed on small fish and plankton. In turn, they are eaten by turtles, crabs and some fish.

Eating plants

Many animals feed on plants, especially the leaves, fruits and roots. These animals are known as herbivores. Herbivores are eaten by meat-eating animals called carnivores. Carnivores are predators because they feed on other animals.

▼ The giraffe is a herbivore. It uses its long tongue to pull leaves off trees.

Catching prey

Predators are usually larger and fewer in number than their prey. They have many different ways of catching it. For example, spiders spin a web of sticky threads to catch flying insects.

Q Which fish fishes for food?

A The angler fish. It has a long spine that sticks out from the middle of its head with a knob at the end. It dangles this to attract small fish, and when they get close the angler fish grabs them in its wide mouth.

long spine to attract small fish

◀ The predator lynx feeds on smaller animals such as pheasants and rabbits.

▲ Angler fish.

Lying in wait

Some predators wait for their prey to come close and then jump out on them. They rely on **camouflage** so that they are not noticed. For example, frogfish have an irregular shape to blend with the rocks and coral on which they rest, while crab spiders are the same colour as the flower in which they hide. Flat fish such as turbot lie just under the surface of the seabed so they cannot be spotted.

Scavengers

When animals die, their bodies become food for other animals called **scavengers**. Without scavengers, the bodies of dead animals would pile up everywhere.

▼ A vulture has excellent eyesight. This means it can spot dead bodies on the ground from far away.

Vultures

Vultures are common scavengers in many countries, where they are seen circling high in the sky. A group of vultures quickly removes all the edible bits of a body, leaving just bits of skin and bone. Some vultures have featherless necks so that they can place their head inside a dead body without their feathers becoming covered in blood and rotting meat.

Small scavengers

Amongst the smaller scavengers are beetles and maggots. Many types of fly lay their eggs on dead bodies so that their larvae, called maggots, have plenty of food. Within a few days all the soft parts of the dead body are gone.

◄ Maggots feed on dead remains and then **pupate**. Adult flies hatch a few days later.

Q and A

▼ Hyenas and jackals scavenge for food on the African **savannah**.

Q Which animal's favourite food is dung?

A The **dung** beetle. Dung beetles' excellent sense of smell allows them to detect dung as soon as it hits the ground, and then there is a race to get to it first. The beetles break off small pieces and roll them along before burying them. Dung is so precious that dung beetles steal the dung balls of other beetles.

▲ Dung beetles.

Bacteria and fungi

These tiny **decomposers** feed on animal dung as well as dead bodies. They release chemicals called enzymes that break down the remains and make them into a liquid. The decomposers absorb, or take up, this liquid. During this process, some of the nutrients from the remains are released into the ground where they are taken up by plant roots. So the cycle begins again.

27

How long do animals live?

Some animals live for just a day or so, but others can live for hundreds of years.

Record breakers

One of the longest-lived animals is the giant tortoise, a type of reptile. Giant tortoises are found on islands such as the Galapagos and Seychelles. Several giant tortoises are known to have lived for 175 years or more. Other animals with long lives include humans and elephants at 70 years, crocodiles at 50 to 70 years and swans that live to more than 100 years of age.

▼ Giant tortoises grow very slowly all through their long life. They can weigh up to 300 kg.

Long cycle

Insects can be long-lived. The cicada, a type of bug, spends up to 17 years as a larva in the ground. Then the adult emerges, breeds and dies within a few weeks.

◀ A cicada has the longest-known life span of any insect.

Heart beats

Usually a smaller mammal has a shorter life than a large mammal. Some scientists think this is to do with the number of times its heart beats. They estimate that a mammal's heart can beat about one billion times. Mice have hearts that beat very fast, so they use up their billion beats in just four years. Elephants have a slow-beating heart and therefore live longer.

▶ Elephants can live for over 70 years.

Q What is the world's oldest animal?

A A clam living in waters off the coast of Norway. This particular clam may be 400 years old. On land, a giant tortoise named Tu'i Malila was believed to have lived to 188 years.

▲ Clam.

Glossary

abdomen the body part of an insect behind the thorax, or lower part of the body of a vertebrate

ammonite a mollusc with a coiled shell that lived in the oceans hundreds of millions of years ago

amoeba a single-celled animal that lives in water

amphibian an animal such as a frog or toad that lives in water and on land

antenna a feeler, used by insects such as butterflies to detect smell

asexual reproduction a form of reproduction where an individual makes a copy of itself, by budding or dividing, without the involvement of another individual

blubber a layer of fat beneath the skin that helps to keep an animal warm

breed to reproduce

camouflage colouring that blends with the background

courtship behaviour such as dancing that some animals perform before mating

crèche a group of young animals left together. Older penguin chicks are left in a crèche while their parents feed

decomposer an organism that breaks down dead and decaying matter

dependent reliant on another

display to show, perform

dung animal droppings

egg the first stage in the life cycle of an animal; the embryo develops within the egg

embryo the first stage of a new life produced when an egg and sperm join together

feature a characteristic, a part of the appearance of an animal

fertilisation the joining together of an egg and sperm

food chain feeding relationships between plants, herbivores and carnivores

gamete the special sex cells made by animals for reproduction

gestation the period of time between fertilisation and birth

incubate to keep eggs warm while the embryo develops inside

invertebrate an animal without a backbone

larva the growing stage of an animal such as an insect

lemur a type of primate found in Madagascar, an island off the east coast of southern Africa

mammal a vertebrate animal that is covered with hair. The female gives birth to live young and feeds them with her own milk

metamorphosis a change in the appearance of an animal in its life cycle

mollusc an invertebrate with a muscular foot and a shell found outside or inside its body, for example snail, octopus and squid

moult when an animal sheds, or gets rid of part of its body, such as old skin, hair or feathers, or when insects and crabs shed their outer skeleton to grow larger

nutrient a substance found in food or in the soil that is needed for organisms to grow

opossum a mammal that carries its young in a pouch, found in North, South and Central America

plankton tiny plants and animals that float in the upper layer of seas and oceans

predator an animal that hunts other animals for food

prey animals that are eaten by predators

primate a type of mammal, for example monkeys and apes

pupa in insects, the stage in the life cycle between larva and adult

pupate when a larva turns into a pupa

reproduce to produce offspring

reptile a vertebrate with a scaly skin

savannah vast plains of grass in Africa

scavenger an animal that feeds on the dead remains of other animals

sea anemone a marine invertebrate with tentacles that are covered in stinging cells

single-celled consisting of just one cell, the building block from which all organisms are composed

skeleton the part of the body that gives support and protection, it may be inside or around the outside of an animal's body

species a group of organisms with the same features that can breed with each other

suckle to suck or drink milk from the mother

vertebrate an animal with a backbone

Further reading

Life cycle of a mammal, Mike Unwin, (Heinemann, 2004)
Ducks and other birds, Sally Morgan, (Chrysalis, 2003)
The Food Cycle, Sally Morgan (Wayland, 2008)
Face to Face with Frogs, Mark Moffett, (National Geographic Society, 2008)

Websites

Life of mammals with interactive challenges: www.bbc.co.uk/nature/animals/mammals/challenges
Life of a butterfly: www.lifeofabutterfly.com/lifecycle.html
Frogs: www.kiddyhouse.com/Themes/frogs

Index

CLICK, CLACK, MOO
Cows That Type

For my Dad – D.C.
To Sue Dooley – B.L.

ARTIST'S NOTE:

For this book I did brush drawings using Windsor Newton lamp black watercolour on tracing paper. I then had the drawings photocopied onto one-ply strathmore kid finish watercolour paper and applied watercolour washes to the black drawings. The advantage to this method is that I can get as many copies on the watercolour paper as I want, and I can experiment with the colour, choosing the finishes that I like best.

SIMON &
SCHUSTER

First published in Great Britain in 2002 by Simon & Schuster UK Ltd
Africa House, 64-78 Kingsway, London WC2B 6AH

Text copyright © 2002 by Doreen Cornin. Illustrations copyright © 2002 by Betsy Lewin

ISBN 0 689 83662 7

Printed in Singapore

1 3 5 7 9 10 8 6 4 2

CLICK, CLACK, MOO
Cows That Type

by Doreen Cronin   pictures by Betsy Lewin

Simon & Schuster

Farmer Brown has a problem.
His cows like to type.
All day long he hears

Click, clack, **moo.**
 Click, clack, **moo.**
Clickety, clack, **moo.**

At first, he couldn't believe his ears.
Cows that type?
Impossible!

Click, clack, **moo.**
Click, clack, **moo.**
Clickety, clack, **moo.**

Then, he couldn't believe his eyes.

Dear Farmer Brown,
The barn is very cold
at night.
We'd like some electric
blankets.
Sincerely,
The Cows

It was bad enough the cows
had found the old typewriter in
the barn, but now they wanted
electric blankets! "No way,"
said Farmer Brown. "No electric
blankets."

So the cows went on strike.
They left a note on the
barn door.

Sorry.
We're closed.
No milk
today.

"No milk today!" cried Farmer Brown. In the background, he heard the cows busy at work:

Click, clack, **moo.**
Click, clack, **moo.**
Clickety, clack, **moo.**

The next day, he got another note:

Dear Farmer Brown,
The hens are cold too.
They'd like electric
blankets.
Sincerely,
The Cows

The cows were growing impatient with the farmer. They left a new note on the barn door.

"No eggs!" cried Farmer Brown. In the background he heard them.

Click, clack, **moo.**
 Click, clack, **moo.**
Clickety, clack, **moo.**

"Cows that type. Hens on strike! Whoever heard of such a thing? How can I run a farm with no milk and no eggs!" Farmer Brown was furious.

Farmer Brown got out his own typewriter.

Dear Cows and Hens:

There will be no electric blankets.
You are cows and hens.
I demand milk and eggs.

Sincerely,
Farmer Brown

Duck was a neutral party, so he brought the ultimatum to the cows.

The cows held an emergency meeting. All the animals gathered around the barn to snoop, but none of them could understand Moo.

All night long, Farmer Brown waited for an answer.

Duck knocked on the door early the next morning. He handed Farmer Brown a note:

Dear Farmer Brown,

We will exchange our typewriter
for electric blankets.
Leave them outside the barn door
and we will send Duck over
with the typewriter.

Sincerely,
The Cows

Farmer Brown decided this was
a good deal. He left the blankets

next to the barn door and waited for
Duck to come with the typewriter.

The next morning he got a note:

Dear Farmer Brown,
The pond is quite boring.
We'd like a diving board.
Sincerely,
The Ducks

Click, clack, **quack.**
Click, clack, **quack.**
Clickety, clack, **quack.**